Animals with Fangs

Written by Michèle Dufresne

PIONEER VALLEY EDUCATIONAL PRESS, INC.

Some **animals** have fangs.

What is a fang?

A fang is a long **tooth**

that can grab on and cling

to an animal's flesh.

Many **snakes** have fangs.
This snake has a very
long fang.

The snake bit its **prey**.
Venom from the snake's fangs
will stop the prey's lungs
and kill it.

A snake's venom can stop
an animal's heart, hurt the
lungs, or make an animal
sleepy, which helps the
snake catch its food.

Spiders also have fangs with venom.

This small bug
is stuck in the spider's web.
The bug's wings are a good
snack for the spider!

This is a black widow. It is one of the most dangerous spiders. If you are bitten by a black widow, its venom can cause severe pain, stiffness, and muscle spasms in your body.

Many big cats have fangs.
This big cat is hunting.

To grab an animal,
the cat jumps up
and uses its long fangs
to bring down its prey.

Lions use their fangs to clamp down on the throat or the neck of their prey. This sometimes helps lions kill animals that are larger than themselves.

Look at the bats hang.
Some bats have fangs.
They use their fangs to cut
into the skin of an animal.

Vampire bats make a small cut with their teeth into an animal and lap up their prey's blood. They feed on cows, pigs, horses, birds, and other animals. They only rarely bite humans.

glossary